A Heart of Gold
The Sticky Mess

TRESCA TRENT GRANNUM

ILLUSTRATED BY
NEFTALI MELENDEZ &
JEREMY WELLS

ISBN; 13: 978-0-9987990-2-5

DEDICATION

I dedicate this book to my Heavenly Papa and my Lord Jesus Christ who chose me as their own before the beginning of time. I am chosen to share their glorious life and love with others. Also, I dedicate this book to my family, especially to my sister Tonyea and my best friend and husband Tony. He has taught me the meaning of faithfulness and loyalty until the end.

Once upon a time in a castle surrounded by golden pillars lived a king, his brother, his elder son, and two young children.

When the children were ages six and seven, the king gave each of them a necklace with a heart of gold. The King said, "Children, here is my heart of gold. It's filled with my love, grace, peace, compassion, and courage. Guard, protect it, and keep it close to your hearts every day of your lives. It will always remind you of who I am and who you are in me." The prince and princess both said, "Yes father, we will."

One day the children were playing near the rear gate of the castle when a six-year-old boy from a faraway village came to the gate. The prince said, "Hello, I have never seen you around here before, are you lost?" The little boy nodded his head, yes.

So the prince and his sister opened the gate. But as soon as they opened the gate, the lost boy's father pushed him to the side and said, "I do not mean to frighten you, I need money to buy food for my son and I."

The prince said, "Our father told us to keep our hearts of gold close to our hearts, never to let them out of our sight!"
But the man replied, "But did your father mean for us to starve? We can trade those hearts for money and buy food for our empty stomachs."

With those words, the prince and princess felt sorry for the man and his son, then the princess said, "We will give them to you so you can eat."
As they were removing the hearts of gold from their necks, the man reached to grab the hearts and they turned into tar.

Suddenly, tar covered them from head to toe. Then, the children panicked, and remembered the words of their father to guard and protect their hearts. The man and his son rushed away laughing when they saw the looks on the prince and princess' faces as they were dripping with tar.

"Quick! Quick! We must do something before our father finds out what we've done," said the prince. "Hurry, we can find a river outside the gate to wash off this black stuff!"

Then the princess said, "Wait! Let's try the tub in the horse stables to wash ourselves."

The princess said, "Maybe if we get soap and scrub them, the tar will come off!" "Good idea!" said the prince. They scrubbed and scrubbed themselves with soap for hours still, nothing happened.

The prince said to the princess, "We must find a river to wash ourselves and the hearts of gold." The two of them ran through the castle gates in search of a river to remove the tar. They looked day and night but couldn't find a river.

By night fall they couldn't remember how to get home. The children shivered as they sat in their royal garments, covered in tar, with their black hearts of gold.

The princess cried, "I want my Papa! I miss my Papa! I am so sorry I disobeyed him and let that bad man grab my heart of gold!" The prince said, "What was I thinking to let my heart of gold become tarnished? I want my Papa!" he cried.

Tired and weary, they fell asleep. They remained lost in the woods for three weeks.

The children learned how to take care of themselves. They caught rabbits and cooked them for food. They also cut down the trees in the forest and made a hut to live in.

Even though they were able to take care of themselves, they were very unhappy together. They argued all of the time over who did the most chores, who forgot to get the water, or who was more caring than the other.

The prince and princess forgot who they were, kind, loving, gentle and caring; their actions showed it.

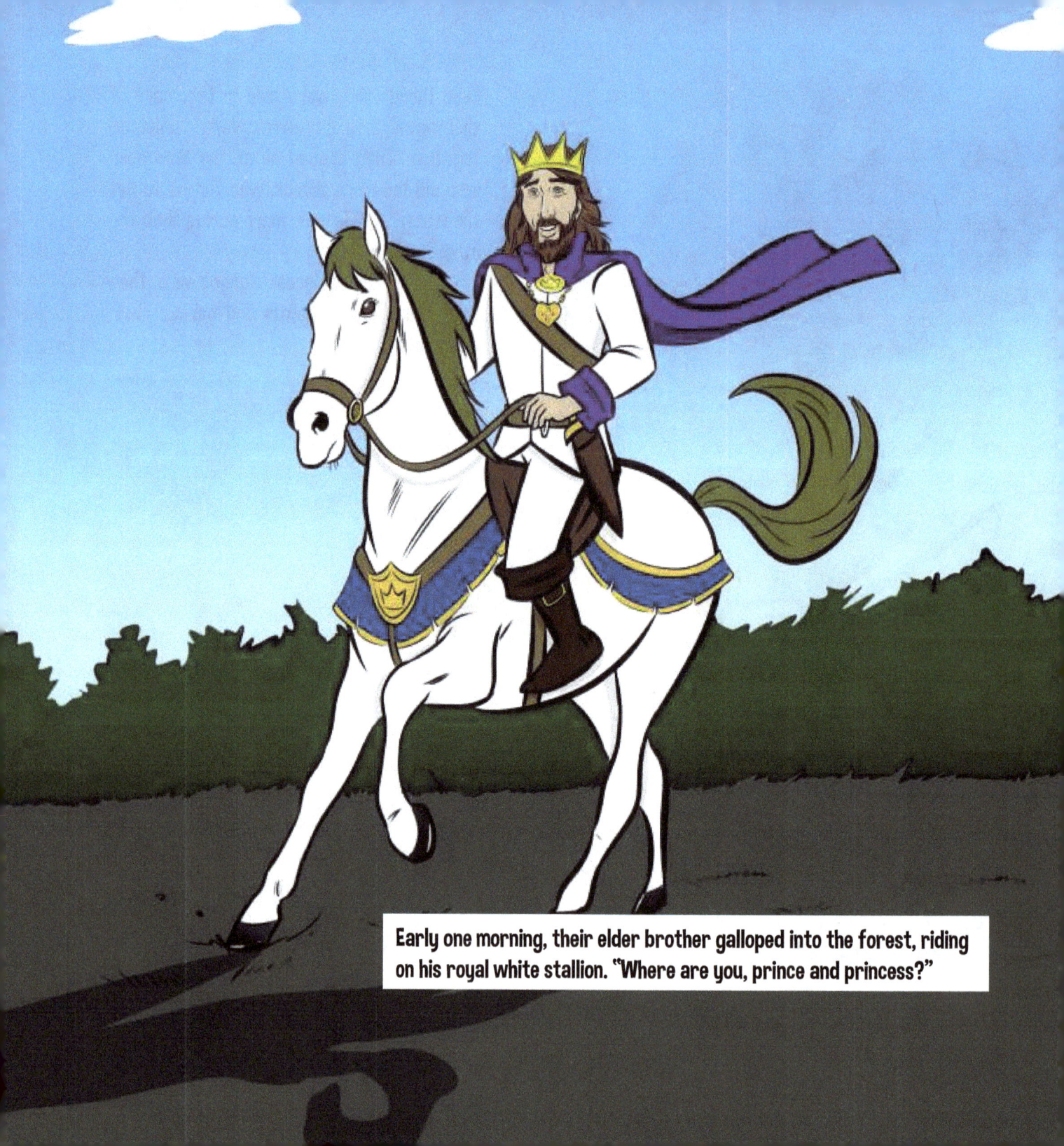

Early one morning, their elder brother galloped into the forest, riding on his royal white stallion. "Where are you, prince and princess?"

"Here we are brother!" yelled the princess.
When their elder brother saw them and their hearts of gold blackened by tar, he grabbed them both in his arms. His white robe became covered with the same tar that covered them.

"We missed you! Dad sent me to find you. I am so grateful you are safe!" he explained.

The prince and princess told their brother how the man and his son tricked them and turned their heart of gold black.

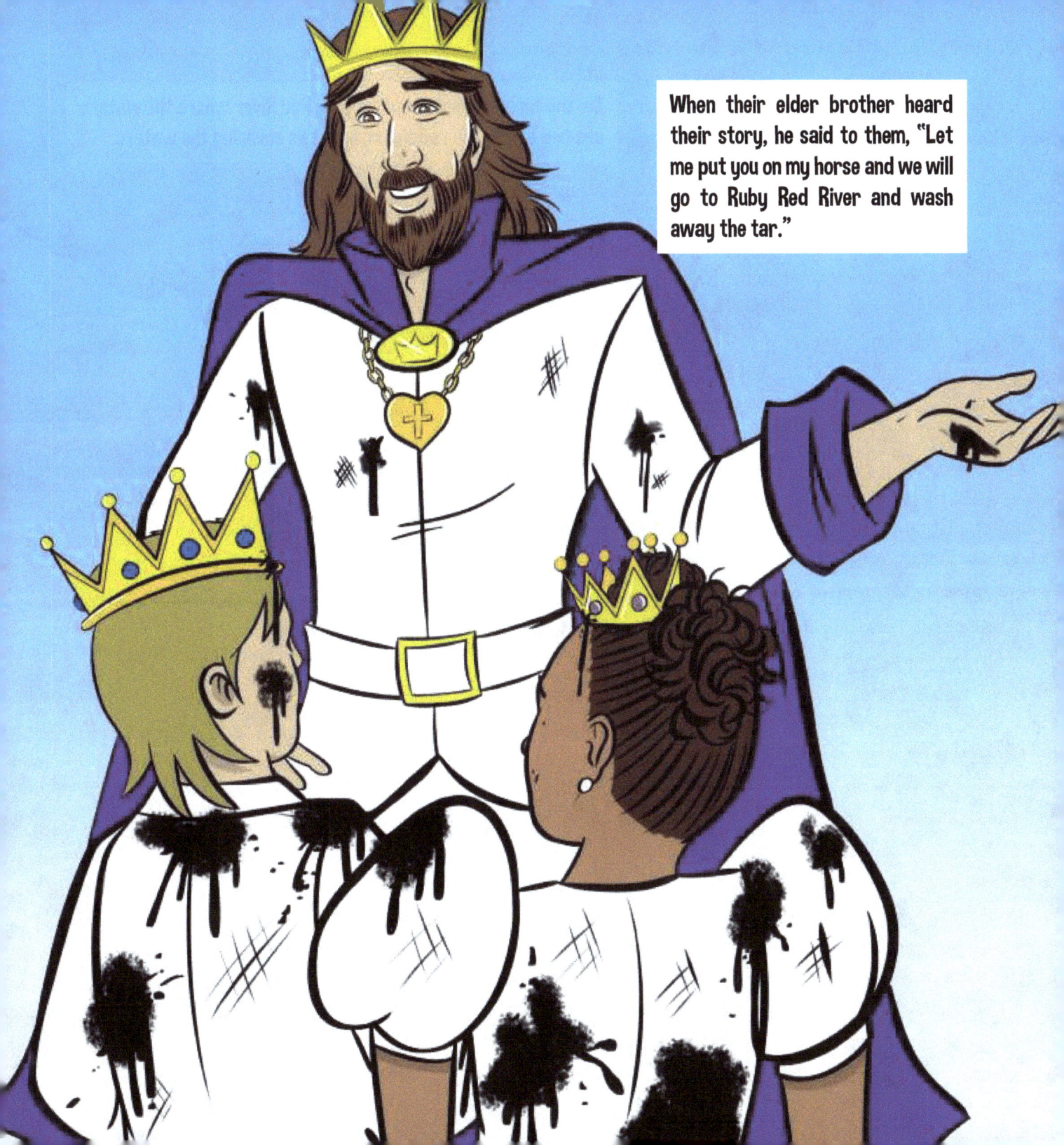

When their elder brother heard their story, he said to them, "Let me put you on my horse and we will go to Ruby Red River and wash away the tar."

So, the three of them went to Ruby Red River where the waters are red due to the reddish rose petals covering the waters.

When they arrived, their elder brother took them from his stallion, washed them and removed the tar from their skin and clothes.

Then he said, "I brought your royal garments from home, let's throw these old tarred clothes away. They put on the garments prepared by their father and a new crown for their heads.

When their elder brother saw their tarred hearts of gold, he said, "We will have to throw these away, they are no longer pure and sacred. Look how they stained your new clothes!"

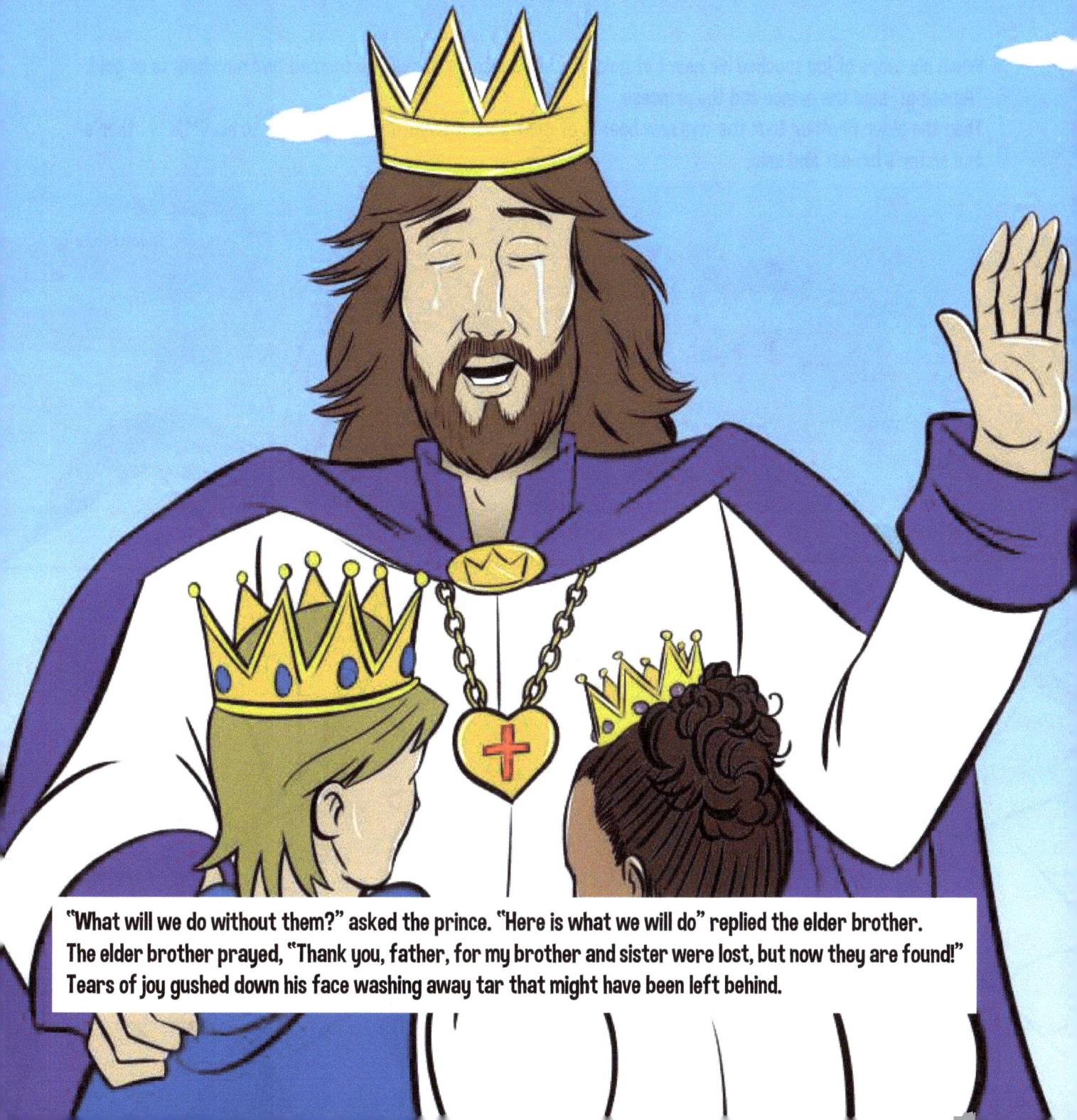

"What will we do without them?" asked the prince. "Here is what we will do" replied the elder brother.
The elder brother prayed, "Thank you, father, for my brother and sister were lost, but now they are found!"
Tears of joy gushed down his face washing away tar that might have been left behind.

When his tears of joy touched his heart of gold, it melted into his hands and formed two new hearts of gold. "Amazing!" said the prince and the princess.
Then the elder brother took the two new hearts of gold, kissed them, and sealed them to his little brother's and sister's breast and said,

Even though the children were eager to go home, they were still wrestling with leaving their hut, old clothes, fishing rod, broom, and other things they used to survive.

"Wait!" said the prince to his elder brother. "There are some things I need to take back home with me." "Me too!" exclaimed the princess. So they gathered their items together and rolled them in a blanket.

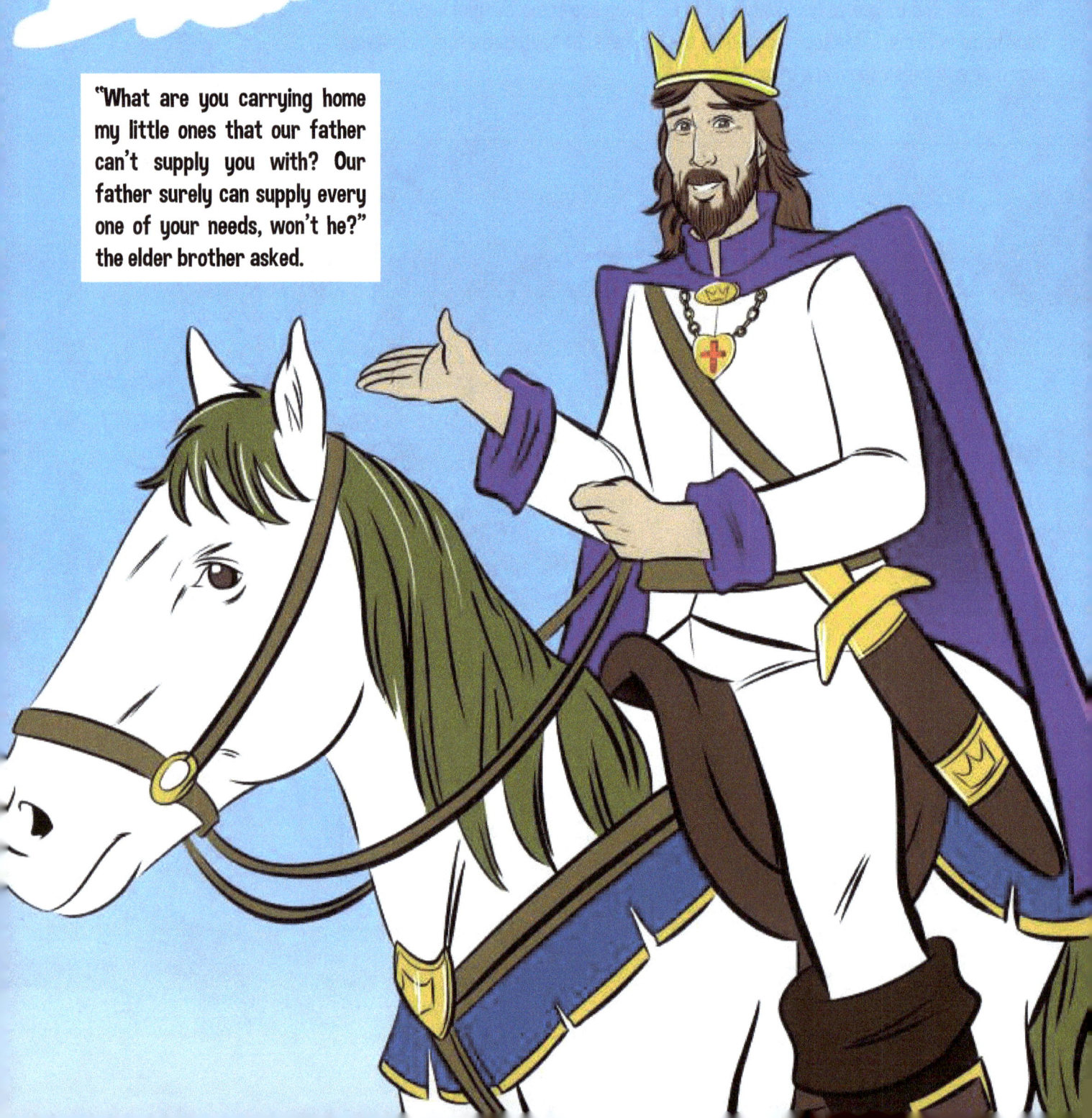

"What are you carrying home my little ones that our father can't supply you with? Our father surely can supply every one of your needs, won't he?" the elder brother asked.

"We want to show our father what we have done and the things we have learned on our own without him, what's wrong with that?" asked the prince.

The elder brother noticed the difference in their attitude and behavior and decided it will be something their father will have to address.

So the three of them finally got on their beautiful white stallion and headed home.

With the children's new found freedom and independent attitudes, will their relationship with their father, elder brother, and uncle be affected? We will find out in our next story.

STUDY GUIDE
A Heart of Gold: The Sticky Mess

Heart of Gold - represents the love of God, the Heart of God, our identity of who we belong to and who we are in character and spirit, the TRUE US. It is an outward sign to the world and each other, *I belong to royalty.*

The Family - The family of God is made up of every color, culture, and nationality. We are all born in the same family, those who have given their lives to the Lord Jesus. Diversity, is very important to our Heavenly Father, for that reason He chose various hues of 'earth-suits' for us to live in while we are here on the earth. A different 'immortal-suit' will be given when we get home, unlike the one we wear in the earth. He said to all of His Beloved children, *"You are fearfully and wonderfully made!"* We must treat everyone with love and respect.

The King - represents **God the Father,** He is wise, kind, strong, valiant, loving, and trustworthy. He is the head of the family. He guides and protects the family in love.

Elder Son - represents **Jesus Christ**, he is kind, gentle, caring, and courageous. The elder son risks his life for His family.
- He leaves His palace in search of His lost brother and sister.
- When He finds them, because of His love for them, He allows Himself to become dirtied by the tar of sin that covered them.
- He forgave them and washed away all the tar from their garments
- He gave them a NEW HEART and sealed it in their breast forever. This represents "the children are claimed as His FOREVER." Saved forever!
- His goal was to heal them and restore them back to the position they had in the family.

Little Prince - All little boys.

Little Princess - All little girls.

Uncle Grace - represents the **Holy Spirit**, wise, and gentle. He is a teacher, comforter, and filled with love and compassion.

Man at the Gate - represents the **evil one and Sin**, all **dressed in black** and **gray** but yet handsome and appealing to the eyes. He deceives the children by luring them to listen to him as he questioned their Father's motives and intents. He never speaks the truth to us, because he is a liar.

Little Boy at the Gate - represents **the flesh** the son of Sin. He always sound like us when he speaks to us. He appeals to us by getting us to figure things out our way without asking our parents or adults for help. His voice in our heads tell us, *"You can do it on your own."* He will always get us in trouble.

The Ruby Red River - is a symbol of 'the blood of Christ' and 'baptism into Christ,' which washed away all the tar away from the children from head to toe, forever.

The Red Cross - is a symbol of Calvary and the blood shed to wash away all of our sins, past, present and future. It is a reminder that we died with Christ and bear our crosses daily with Him.

Black Tar - represents **sin**. Sin is what the children received when they listened to the evil one at the gate. Every time we do something against our parent's wishes, hurt someone, or do something that we shouldn't, sin dirties our beautiful garments our Father gave us.

Sin, was responsible for them being mean to each other and not getting along in the woods. Sin caused anger, fear, sadness, loneliness, worry, and their anxieties.

But, when we admit that we are sorry and turn to Jesus who lives *within us*, He cleanses us from all our sin. He already forgave us at the Ruby Red River.

Items in the Woods *(broom, stone hammer, etc.):* **Fleshly Patterns** - *(Means to care for ourselves)* Children's ways of caring for themselves without God. The children learned to be independent, therefore, when it was time to go home, they didn't want to leave their newly found freedom behind. They took the items home, even though their elder brother told them their Father would care for them and meet all of their needs.

The flesh and sin is not who we are, but what we may choose to do.

Tresca Trent Grannum grew up in Holley Homes Projects located in Albany, Georgia. She was raised by a single parent along with her sister Tonyea (Monk). Life was very difficult for them, but her mother's determination and perseverance as a nurse's aide then as a registered nurse administrator afforded them the opportunity to move from the Projects to a different environment. However, the sexual abuse and 25 other traumatic experiences had taken their toll on Tresca. Tresca hid her posttraumatic stress disorder and dissociative identity disorder through activities such as cheerleading, singing, dancing, and acting in school plays-her means to survive. Lost and desperate for healing, she gave her life to her Lord Jesus Christ in 1979. Jesus, told her, "I will restore your soul." Jesus has and is keeping His promise. For the past 35 years, as a pastoral counselor, psychotherapist, and teacher, Tresca has given her whole heart to Christ as He has ministered to others from ages 2 to 80 years to bring hope and healing from their pain and emotional struggles.

Now retired from psychotherapy she continues serving others as a Pastoral Counselor. Even though she has brain aneurysms, brain atrophy, and PTSD she ministers to others through her blog, hispreciousgift.com, song writing and through her books. Tresca presently lives in Ponte Vedra, Florida.

Visit Tresca on her website at www.selahwithlove.com and her blog at www.hispreciousgift.com

Thanks to my illustrators: Nefatali Perez (sketches) and Jeremy Wells (coloring/lines)

www.ingramcontent.com/pod-product-compliance
Lightning Source LLC
Chambersburg PA
CBHW062007090426
42811CB00005B/775